CONTENTS

Cover photo by Harry V. Lacey

Photography
All photographs by Harry V. Lacey, except those listed below.
Al Barry: 46; Walter Pieschel: 20, 32; G.J. Timmerman: 43; Louise Van der Meid: 25, 34, 47, 54, 58, 59, 62; Vogelpark Walsrode: 78, 86.

ISBN 0-87666-753-1

Distributed in the U.S. by T.F.H. Publications, Inc., 211 West Sylvania Avenue, PO Box 427, Neptune, NJ 07753; in England by T.F.H. (Gt. Britain) Ltd., 13 Nutley Lane, Reigate, Surrey; in Canada to the pet trade by Rolf C. Hagen Ltd., 3225 Sartelon Street, Montreal 382, Quebec; in Southeast Asia by Y.W. Ong, 9 Lorong 36 Geylang, Singapore 14; in Australia and the South Pacific by Pet Imports Pty. Ltd., P.O. Box 149, Brookvale 2100, N.S.W. Australia; in South Africa by Valid Agencies, P.O. Box 51901, Randburg 2125 South Africa. Published by T.F.H. Publications, Inc., Ltd, the British Crown Colony of Hong Kong.

all about canaries

by irene evans, Irene

supplemental material
by paul paradise

color photography by
harry v. lacey

A variegated buff Yorkshire.

Opposite:
A variegated buff Yorkshire. The word *buff* refers
to the feathers, which are smaller and placed
closer together than on non-buff varieties.

A pair of Norwich Canaries. The one on the left is of normal coloration,
the one on the right is a brown variegated.

Desirability of Birds in the Home

Birds have been regarded for centuries as the most delightful creatures of nature, and no music is sweeter than the beautiful song of a Canary in your home. The warm color of their plumage, their graceful motions, their peculiar habits and manners as well as their song possess charm that wins the most indifferent. They win the hearts of all who love beauty, grace and sweetness. Years ago Wordsworth wrote:

> *The birds around me hopped and played,*
> *Their thoughts I cannot measure;*
> *But the least motion which they made*
> *It seemed a thrill of pleasure.*

A dark, dreary house seems to come alive when a Canary begins to sing. A palace becomes a home when a Canary becomes one of its occupants.

A Canary is a wonderful companion for elderly people. If they are lonely it brings them companionship. It gives them something to love and to love them in return. It gives them responsibility in caring for the bird, something, perhaps, they have been missing since their family had grown and no longer needed them.

I have known people with nervous breakdowns or imaginary ills who became interested in Canaries and forgot their troubles. One lady told me that she had been going to the doctor several times a week when she became interested in Canaries. She said that after that she forgot to go to the doctor; in fact she didn't need to anymore!

Children are always interested in birds and a Canary in their home becomes one of the family. When they can share in care of the bird it teaches them dependability and reliability.

I have heard folks say that they didn't like to see a bird in a cage. If the cage is right and their needs are properly taken care of, they are happy. They have been born and bred in captivity for centuries and could not live free in nature any longer.

Origin and History

Birds are bipeds, covered with feathers, a covering no other Earth creature has. Nearly all birds have the power of flight. The feathers, which serve as clothing, also assist in flying, protect from heat and cold and create their beauty.

The earliest traces of existence of birds in the world are supposed to be bird tracks found in sandstone in the Connecticut Valley. Fossil birds have been found in New Jersey, Kansas and Idaho. A fossil bird with teeth has been found in Kansas. An extinct bird of New Zealand has been found in fossil deposits; it had legs and feet nearly as massive as those of an elephant. Skeletons of some of these birds may be seen at the Museum of Natural History in New York.

The Canary was native to the Canary Islands and was a small grayish-green bird. History tells us that in the Sixteenth Century sailors trapped many of these birds to take home to Italy. The sailors were shipwrecked near the island of Elba, but finally some of these birds reached Italy. They immediately became popular and from there spread to Germany and England, hence, all over the world.

From these little green birds have been developed all the varieties of Canaries we know today. Mutations have been recognized and sports developed and crosses made with other Finches so that definite standard varieties have been established.

A green Gloster Fancy hen and her brood. New-born chicks eat tremendous amounts of food relative to their size.

A variegated buff Norwich Canary. *Variegation* refers to the natural proportion of light and dark coloration.

A Border Fancy Canary. All *type* Canaries were produced by selective breeding of mutations arising within broods of normal Canaries.

The stout, compact body of this variegated buff Norwich Canary gives it a cuddly appearance.

A pair of Gloster Fancy Canaries with the consort, or plainhead, on the left and the corona, or crested, on the right.

Opposite:
A Border Fancy Canary showing an unvariegated yellow color.

Varieties of Canaries

Hervieux, writing in England over two hundred years ago, mentions twenty-nine varieties of Canaries, among them white, blond, crested, etc. By selective breeding through the years, the song, type and colors have become fixed in the various Canaries.

We can divide Canaries into three categories today:

1. *Roller Canaries* — Raised and trained for song.
2. *Color Bred* or *Red Factor Canaries* — Raised primarily for color and conformation but admired for song also.
3. *Type Canaries* — Raised for special factors of size, shape and various song qualities.

I will mention and describe a few of the most popular varieties that may be seen in Canary shows and pet shops today.

NORWICH CANARY

The Norwich Canary is at least six and one-half inches long. Its head is large and round with a small beak, its neck is short and full, its feathers soft and silky. Its color may be yellow, green, white or cinnamon or with variegations of these colors. It has been called the teddy-bear of the Canaries and will give you the feeling that you would like to cuddle it. It makes a nice cage bird but needs a large cage.

The Norwich was developed by the shoe workers of England in the district called Norwich. It is interesting to read of these shoe workers working long hours at their benches with their Norwich Canaries in back of their work benches where they could watch them and care for them at intervals. It must have made the long hours of their work go much faster.

YORKSHIRE CANARY

This bird is the largest of the Canaries, being almost eight inches long, with a slender body. Its feathers are short, tight and silky, with a very beautiful feather texture. Its colors are yellow, green, white or cinnamon or a variegation of these colors. This bird must be kept in a large cage. The Yorkshire Canary was developed a long time ago by the woolen workers in Yorkshire, England, hence its name.

The large size and slender body build of Yorkshire Canaries make them stand out in a crowd.

Canary hobbyists like variety among their birds. These Norwich Canaries show a number of degrees of variegation and will make excellent breeding stock.

Well loved for its singing ability, the Border Fancy comes in many variegations of color.

BORDER FANCY CANARY

This is a nice, well built bird about six and one-half inches long. It is a round bird with very beautiful glossy plumage. Its color may be yellow, green, white, cinnamon or a variegation of these colors. It sings a variety of songs and makes a very good cage bird if you desire a good robust song. These birds were developed near the border of England and Scotland and for a number of years were called by various names. After much controversy the name Border Fancy was adopted.

LIZARD CANARY

This is one of the oldest known of the type birds. It originated in France. It is a very striking bird, but not seen too much, because it very nearly became extinct during the war. Much interest has been taken in it over the last few years, so it is hoped that they will become more plentiful soon. They are about five and one-half inches long. The best specimens have a yellow cap on the head. The body color is a rich bronzy green. Down the back are rows of shell-like markings called *spangles*. On the breast are smaller rows called *rowing*. The wings, tail, beak and feet are dark—almost black. If or when these birds become plentiful, many people will want them for house birds because they present a very striking picture as well as being good lively birds.

A buff Gloster Fancy corona cock showing its distinctive crest.

The Lizard Canary, well known for spangles and rowing, shell-like markings on the back and breast, respectively.

Norwich Canary. The ideal bird of this breed is judged primarily by the head, which should be large and well rounded, and proportionate to the rest of the body.

The Dutch Frill Canary is a long, slender bird with feathers that seem to curl in the wrong direction.

Opposite:
A clear-cap Lizard Canary. This ancient breed was almost lost and at the end of World War II only a few dozen were left alive.

Opposite:
The dimorphic Red Factor hen has only a trace
of orange visible. This is inherited from the red
siskin used in Canary-siskin crosses to produce
the Red Factor varieties.

The crest of a Gloster Fancy showing a definite
center from which all the crest feathers radiate.
The crest lies neatly, with no irregularities, and it
looks like a cap.

GLOSTER FANCY CANARY

This bird is becoming more popular as it becomes more plentiful. They are very similar to the Border Fancy but smaller. They carry a crest on their head that looks like a little round hat. I should note that not all have the crest but are called "consort" when the crest is not visible. They make good all-around cage birds.

DUTCH FRILL CANARY

This bird isn't seen too often but makes a striking appearance when seen. It is a long, slender bird with long silky

A pair of baby Gloster Fancy Canaries with their distinctive crest. They make good all-around cage birds.

feathers curling around in such a way that they seem to be growing the wrong way. We are told that exhibitors of these birds had special combs and brushes to groom these birds so the curls would lie in just the right direction.

RED FACTOR or COLOR BRED CANARY

The last forty years has seen the development of this bird. It is the only bird that we can claim as having been developed to its point of perfection in the United States. It has been developed by crossing the Venezuelan Black Capped Red Siskin with the Roller and Border Fancy Canaries. The Venezuelan Siskin is a small bird with orange-red body, black wings and cap. Many crosses with other finches have been tried, but this cross has been the only one to consistently breed crosses which in turn are fertile. (Note: the male birds from this cross are nearly always fertile with other Canaries.) By selective breeding from this cross the beautiful colors of near red, red-orange and orange birds have been developed. It is usually about five and one-half inches long. It may be a clear color bird or it may carry variegation. Some are frosted and some are non-frost. By frosting we mean the feathers are each edged with a tiny edging of white that gives the frosted appearance. The feather is a little longer than on the non-frost bird, thus giving the bird a larger, softer appearance. Their song is a combination of rolls, warbles and some of the wild song inherited from the Siskin ancestor. They are variously called warblers, choppers, etc. They make the most popular all-around cage bird today. The last ten years have seen the development of a Top Knot Red Factor. The feathers make a stand up cap on the head of the bird. Often this cap is dark colored on a clear color bird and is very effective.

ROLLER CANARY

Last, but best, comes the opera singer of the bird world, the Roller Canary. They have been bred and trained to a high degree of perfection in the Hartz Mountains of Germany for several centuries. A good, well trained Roller is a delight to hear. They are about five and one-half to six inches long and can be had in yellow, green, white or a variegation of these colors. If one wishes a low pitched, deep toned singer these birds make the best house bird.

Opposite:

A Yorkshire Canary, self-cinnamon. The term *self* refers to a bird in which the dark pigments are solid throughout and no light feathering is visible.

The color which a Red Factor Canary inherits from its siskin ancestors is often enhanced by the practice of color feeding.

Various other Finches including Bull Finch, Linnet and Gold Finch have been crossed with Canaries. They make interesting oddities and some are quite good singers. They have never been developed to any standard because the hybrid crosses from these matings have always proved infertile, and thus cannot be carried on.

COLOR IN THE CANARY

Canaries' colors are derived from pigmentation. There are three basic pigments: yellow, black and brown. Combinations of these pigments result in different colorations of the Canary. *Variegation* refers to the natural proportion of dark and light pigments on the body; it is determined by genes. One group of

Also known as warblers and choppers because of their song, Red Factors have long been popular cage birds.

A Red Factor, frosted rose pastel. The frosted variety of this mutation is even paler than the nonfrosted.

genes determines which areas the pigments will occupy, and another set determines which color will be exhibited.

Pigments are supplied by food sources. Basic yellow, known as lipochrome, comes from greenstuffs and egg yolk. Black and brown, known as melanins, are formed by proteins.

The yellow, or lipochrome, serves as a basic ground color upon which other colors are superimposed. One exception occurs in the group of birds known as buffs. Buffs are paler because of a reduction in yellow pigment. They also have evolved structural differences and have more and thicker feathers. In the buffs the yellow pigment stops short of the outer margin of each feather, leaving a thin white edging known as frosting.

The Roller Canary, world-famous for the beauty of its song. It took several centuries of breeding in Germany to produce such a bird.

General Care

SELECTION

The various kinds of Canaries have already been described. One's own wishes and likes should be the deciding factor in deciding which variety of bird should become a new member of one's family.

If one likes color and a good all-around song then the color bred Canary is the best and the most available in pet shops all over the country. If one is more interested in a low pitched, beautifully toned singer, then the Roller Canary should be chosen. These are usually readily available in most pet shops. If one wishes something different and out of the usual, one of the type birds should be investigated. Not many pet shops keep these birds, but your pet dealer can probably procure them for you if you make your wishes known to him.

When selecting a bird pick a young one that looks in good condition. Feathers should be clean and well groomed. He should be alert and eyes should be bright. A bird who sets with his feathers drooped, perhaps with his head under his wing in the daytime, is not a well bird and will only bring you grief.

Perhaps I should mention that only male birds in the Canary world make good singers. Occasionally a female bird will sing a little but not a continuing, connected song.

Only an experienced bird handler can tell by sight what the sex of a Canary is. Generally the male is more bold, and his song is sweet and has a ring to it. Compared to that of the male, the song of the female is like a warble, if she sings at all. Also, the female does not hold herself up as the male does.

If you want a male canary it is best to buy only from a reliable pet dealer. Canary breeders will sometimes try to sell extra females as males to unwary customers.

An apricot Red Factor hen. The color is lightly frosted throughout.

The body type of Crested Canaries, like this Crestbred, derives from Norwich stock.

A reliable pet dealer will give you a written guarantee that the Canary is a male. The guarantee should also state in writing that the bird will sing and that if the bird does not sing the purchaser can return the bird for a refund. The time limit for singing is usually fourteen days.

The pet dealer will stamp the wings of the bird with indelible ink. This is for his protection, to insure that if the bird is returned it is the same one he has guaranteed. The ink will fade within a month when the bird sheds. Naturally, with all these precautions male Canaries cost considerably more than the females.

In a clean, well kept pet shop the attendant can be of great help in making your selection. He will become acquainted with the alert good singing bird and can give you good advice.

METABOLISM

Canaries have a much faster metabolism than human beings and other mammals. For instance, the human heart beats 70 to 80 times a minute, but a Canary's heart beats 800 to 1,000 times a minute. Holding a Canary in your hand is like holding a small motor: you can feel the heart beating rapidly. Canaries do not have pores to regulate temperature and can not sweat. They cool themselves by breathing with the mouth open and drinking cool water. Also, the feathers can be held in or puffed up to act as insulation. Puffing up the feathers allows air to penetrate to the skin surface; compressing the feathers tightly creates a dead-air space for warmth. The body temperature of a Canary, 109° F., is higher than that of human beings. To keep its higher metabolism going requires much food: the average Canary weighs only two-thirds of an ounce yet eats one-eighth of an ounce of food daily, a high ratio of amount consumed to amount weighed.

This baby Gloster Fancy Canary depends on its feathers, which will become more profuse after it sheds, to maintain its body heat.

Two Border Fancy Canaries; the one on the right is a self green.

A clear yellow Yorkshire hen.

DIGESTION

One very important fact about a Canary's beak is that it contains no teeth. After a few feedings, the Canary will have left many seed husks in the cage. The Canary husks the seed with its beak and swallows the grain whole. The grain passes into the throat and is held in storage in the crop. In the throat is the esophagus, and this stretches to store food. From the crop the grain passes into a glandular stomach, where it is moistened by digestive enzymes that help break it down. From the glandular stomach the seed passes into the gizzard, a muscular stomach containing gravel. The stomach muscles grind the seed against the gravel just as seed is ground up in a mill. The resulting mass passes into the intestines, where it is absorbed for nutrients. Grayish brown or black waste is later excreted.

PREENING

All birds preen, and this is a joy to behold. The bird will fluff up its feathers and shake them. It will sort through its feathers with its beak or, after flapping its wings vigorously, will pull the wing feathers through the beak to rearrange them. At the point of attachment of the long tail feathers is a small oil gland called the uropygial gland. The bird will obtain a small supply of oil from this gland and rub it on its feathers and feet as part of the preening behavior. This adds a gloss to the bird's appearance as well as protection from the elements in nature.

HOLDING A CANARY

At some time your Canary may escape, so you should know how to catch and hold him. To hold your Canary, wait until his wings are in their natural position, then place your palm around his back and hold his feathers in place with your fingertips. In this way you will not risk crushing him or cutting off his breath. Nor will he be able to flap, because the pressure of your grip is over the more-sturdy wing. If your canary should escape, you should grasp him in that manner. Before trying to catch him, make sure all fans or oven burners are turned off, and any cats or dogs removed. A tame Canary should be fairly easy to catch, though he may fly around. Move slowly and you will not alarm your pet. For a difficult to reach place you may use a perching stick rather than trying to dislodge the bird. A perching stick is a slender pole with a vertical perch attached. They can be bought at most pet stores.

TEACHING TRICKS

Birds are not known to display great intelligence, but teaching your Canary a trick or two can go right alongside taming him. Canaries have a natural fear of movement, especially over-head movement. With patience, you can teach your Canary to perch on your hand. Remove the perch and set the

This Canary is being administered a vitamin solution. This is the correct way to hold a canary.

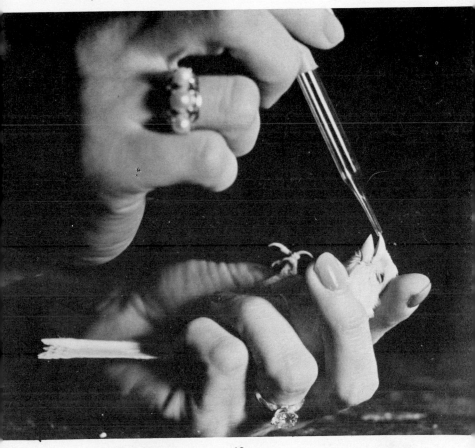

This Border Fancy is a self blue. The 'blue' color is more gray or brown than blue.

A Border Fancy. One of the smaller Canaries, the Border Fancy attains a maximum size of six to six and one-half inches.

cage on a table until you are at eye-level with your pet. Insert a pencil or finger inside and try gently to induce the bird to perch. This usually requires some effort, and the first few tries you should coax him for no more than a few minutes. Eventually the bird should start perching on your finger and can be taught to eat seed or some treat from your finger. Pet stores sell carts and cars especially designed for birds. As the bird pecks at the seed inside, the cart moves. A Canary that can be taught to perch on your finger can be induced to eat from these toy carts.

Pet stores sell safe, movable carts and cars that your canary can be trained to eat seed from.

Training a canary to perch on your hand is relatively easy to do with some patience on your part. A canary can be trained to eat seed from your hand.

FOOD AND FEEDING

First of all, the seed you feed your bird must be clean and fresh and constant. They eat a great many times a day. The old adage of 'eating like a Canary bird' should be interpreted as an insult. If humans ate as much as a Canary in proportion to their size I am sure they would soon weigh half a ton.

Dirty, dusty seed can be the source of much trouble with birds. Old seed becomes rancid, which creates more trouble. **Canary seed** is the 'bread and butter' of the Canary diet. It is a bright yellowish colored seed, rounded in the middle and pointed at the ends. It provides muscle (nitrogen), heat (car-

One of the newest mutations in the Red Factor Canary, the bronze ino rose pastel.

Opposite, upper photo:
A frosted rose pastel Red Factor Canary.

Opposite, lower photo:
A roller Canary in her breeding nest. Nesting material is provided during mating, and the hen will build the nest herself.

bon), phosphorus and iron for vigor as well as fibre. Its composition is: protein 13.5, fat 4.9, carbohydrates 51.6, ash 2.1, water 13.6.

Rape seed is added to the Canary seed usually about two parts Canary to one part rape seed. It is a small, brownish-black, round seed. It is rich in magnesium, lime, potash and phosphoric acid. When you buy rape seed chew up a few grains. They should be sweet and nutty tasting. If they taste bitter and biting it is not good seed. Its composition is: protein 9.4, fat 40.5, carbohydrates 10.2, ash 3.9, water 11.5.

Next in importance is **grit**. When a bird eats, the food enters the crop where the grit acts as a grinding agent. Good

Shortly after hatching, young chicks will be eating rape seed. The seed should be soaked in water and given to the hen to feed the chicks.

sharp grit mixed with various minerals is good for birds. A supply should always be available in every cage. All seed companies now carry good mineral grit.

Niger seed is a shiny, elongated, almost black seed. It is an oily stimulating seed, which maintains health, enriches plumage and restores song. Its composition is: protein 17.5, fat 32.7, carbohydrates 15.3, ash 7.0, water 8.4.

Poppy or **maw seed** is a small gray seed. It corrects constipation and diarrhea conditions and is readily digestible. Its composition is: protein 17.5, fat 40.3, carbohydrates 12.2, ash 5.8, water 14.6.

Flax or **linseed** is a pointed reddish colored seed. This seed gives gloss to the plumage and is especially good during the moult.

There are many more supplementary seeds such as teasle, sesame, oat groats, anise, etc. All pet stores now carry good mixtures of "treat" seed which contain a mixture of these seeds. A small amount of these should be fed every day. The bird will eat what it needs of them.

A good clean piece of cuttle bone should be in every cage at all times. It furnishes minerals and vitamins and helps to keep the beak in good condition. As added food a variety may be given on different days. For instance, a piece of hard boiled egg one day, a piece of apple or orange the next day, etc.

Every bird needs some greens every day, the darker the green the better. Kale, romaine lettuce or spinach are good greens. If you have clean dandelions in your yard there is nothing better. If you cannot obtain fresh greens there is available in pet shops a packaged dried green that is good. I also saw an interesting article in one of our pet shops. It was a little plastic dish to hang in the cage planted with seed ready to grow when water was added. I understand that new cartridges of seed are available when the first one is used up. Small flower pots can be planted with rape seed that will sprout in a few days. The flower pot can be set in the cage. The rape greens are very good food.

I have heard people say that greens give their birds diarrhea. This is because they give it just once in a while. The bird is so hungry for it he eats too much, just as a child will make him-

Red Factor red orange.

A wing-marked Border Fancy with the marked wing visible. The marked wing is differently colored than the rest of the bird's body.

self sick on candy if given free rein. If the bird has his greens every day he will adjust himself to the amount he needs. If your bird has not been having greens, then start with just a small amount at first.

HOUSING

A good-sized metal cage is best for birds. They are easier to clean and do not provide the hiding places for mites that other types of cages do.

The cage should be hung about six feet from the floor in a light airy room. The airy room does not mean in a draft. There is no easier way to make a bird sick than to leave it in a draft. The temperature should be between sixty and seventy degrees

Birds sleep at night, and the cage should be covered to keep out drafts of cold air.

as much as possible. Birds can stand extremes of heat and cold; it is sudden extreme changes that do much harm. Extreme heat makes him go into a soft moult which will make him stop singing and if continued will eventually kill him. Too much tobacco fumes and gas fumes are very dangerous. Fresh paint odors can kill him in a short time.

It is natural for a bird to go to sleep soon after sundown, so if he is in a place where the lights are kept on late, at least cover his cage.

The cage should be as large as possible and the perches arranged so that the bird may exercise by flying back and forth between them.

The cage must be kept clean. If not, the bird cannot keep himself clean and dirt in his food will affect his health. The cage should be washed at intervals. The bottom of the cage should be covered with paper. Newspapers tend to rub off on the bird and give him a dirty appearance. Pet shops have a gravel paper that can be used.

Perches should be cleaned often. There are brushes made for this purpose. If the perches are washed they should be thoroughly dried, for a damp perch will give the bird rheumatism. The perches should be oval, with cut sides. Small round perches are cruel and in time will cause much foot trouble.

The seed and water dishes should be kept clean at all times and occasionally sterilized.

Just a few minutes a day does all this and really pays off with a good looking, healthy, happy bird. Only happy, healthy birds sing.

Most birds like a bath every day and will have much better looking feather texture if they have it. The water should be cool but not too cold. Different birds like different kinds of bath dishes. There is a bath dish that fits on the door of the cage. Some prefer a small tub or saucer inside. If the bird doesn't at first take a bath keep offering it, and perhaps sprinkle him a little to get him started. Experiment with your bird to find out his preferences.

A bird loves some sunlight but never, never leave him in the sun where he cannot get out of it. I have known of birds being killed by being left in too much sun with no way to

A green Gloster Fancy whose crest radiates well.

Opposite:
Crested Canaries. The bird on the right has a
visibly well developed crest and is called a "crest."
The other lacks the crest and is referred to as
"crestbred."

escape. Never set him so the sun shines on him through glass. This can be very bad for him and his feathers. Don't hang your bird outside at the mercy of the sun, wind and stray cats. Whenever I see a bird hanging outside in a cage I am tempted to stop and tell the owner how stupid and cruel it is.

If you are so situated that you can let your bird out for a little while to fly about the room it is good for him.

When I was a child we had a Canary for a good many years. The door of his cage was never closed. He slept in it at night and visited it at intervals during the day for food, a sip of water, a bath or a short nap. My mother had an old fashioned kitchen cabinet. A shiny alarm clock was kept on the top of this. Right along side of the alarm clock was where he spent much of his day. Whether it was the ticking of the clock that kept him company or the shiny surface where he could see himself, we could never decide. Most of his singing was done in the cage, but he had little sweet noises he made to the clock.

Your Canary should be provided with a bird bath, which he will probably use every day. The water should not be too cold.

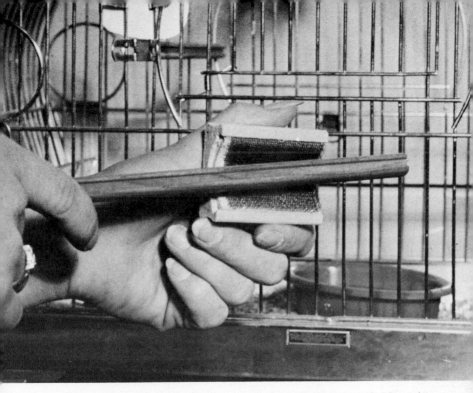

Brushes to clean the perch will save a lot of work. They can be bought at most pet shops.

HEALTH CARE AND REMEDIES

If a bird is well fed, well housed and kept clean there is very little need for medicine and remedies.

If one is buying a bird they should be sure they are buying a healthy bird and then take care to keep it that way. Very often when a person realizes his bird is sick it is too late to help it. An alert, smooth feathered, bright-eyed bird that is singing is a healthy bird.

If you suspect something is wrong it is best to consult a reliable pet shop or a veterinarian who is interested in birds. They will have various tonics, antibiotics, etc., that may save your pet. If its illness has reached chronic stages don't expect them to be able to help much.

Some of the commonest ailments are as follows:

Asthma — This, as with humans, affects the breathing of

A buff Yorkshire Canary.

A cinnamon variegated buff Yorkshire.

the bird, and can cause wheezing. It usually comes from the dust in unclean seed. In the early stage a couple of drops of iodine in the water may help. Some folks use a tiny amount of Vicks in the nostril or even in the beak. This is especially helpful if a tiny piece of seed hull has become lodged there.

Rheumatism — Usually is caused by damp perches or from being left in a draft.

Diarrhea — Usually caused by wrong feeding or overfeeding of food that the bird is not in the habit of eating. A pinch of Sal Hepatica in the water may correct the condition. A dish of

A fancy bird cage for several canaries.

Cages should be roomy enough
to allow your Canary freedom of
motion. At least two perches
should be provided.

Eighteen-day-old Gloster Fancy Canaries about to leave the nest.

poppy seed or poppy seed sprinkled on a piece of bread dipped in milk is very good for this condition.

Toe-nails too long — As the bird gets older, sometimes the nails grow very long and give the bird trouble holding the perch. Unless they are really bad they should be left long. In case they are bad they should be trimmed. Hold the foot up to the light. You can see the little vein running into the nail. Use nail clippers to cut the end of the nail but do not cut into the vein or the bird will bleed.

Beak too long — Occasionally the beak on an older bird grows too fast and will interfere with its cracking seed. For this condition it is wisest to consult an expert as this is a rather delicate job and needs someone with experience.

Broken feathers — If a tail or wing feather becomes broken it should be gently pulled out. A blood vein runs into the feather and the bird can soon bleed to death if not attended to.

Scaly feet — This condition is usually caused by a tiny scale mite which gets under the scales of the feet. The feet develop hard scales and can become red and inflamed. They should be gently soaked in warm soapy water, dried and ointment applied. In a few treatments the scales will easily rub off. Perches and cage should be sterilized if this condition is present.

Red mites — This is one of the worst pests of the bird world. It doesn't seem to make much difference how clean a bird and its surroundings are kept, it will sometimes develop a siege of mites. I have been told that they can come in the seed. One should always be on the watch for them because a bird will not stay healthy and happy if they are present. If a bird continually picks itself, perhaps seems to look puffy and maybe quits singing, you should suspect red mites. At night place a clean white cloth over the cage. In the morning the cloth will show little red dots if mites are present. The cage should be thoroughly disinfected. The ends of the perches and crevices in the cage should be painted with a good mite liquid or sprayed thoroughly with mite spray. The mites stay on the bird only at night and hide in crevices in the daytime. A few treatments will rid you of them.

Moult — It is normal and natural for a bird to moult in the

A well-matched breeding pair of Gloster Fancy Canaries; a buff consort cock and a white corona hen.

summer time. It usually takes from six to eight weeks to finish. Most birds do not sing much, if at all, at this time and they should receive extra good care. If possible, keep them in a quiet, warm (but not too hot) place; keep them well fed, and give plenty of baths.

It should be remembered that it is quite a process for them to grow all new feathers in a few weeks time, and while normal, is still a strain on the bird's health.

There is no reason for a healthy, well cared for bird to stop singing. If your bird stops singing look for the reason.

Is he well cared for?

Is he by any chance in a draft?

Is his food clean and fresh?

Is his water clean?

Could he have red mites?

There are some excellent books on bird diseases. Read one.

This clear-capped gold Lizard male shows good breast markings.

Breeding the Canary

Any beginner who wants to start breeding Canaries should first know something about their biology. After this he should decide on whether to breed for color or for singing, as to do both at the same time is impracticable. It would not be advisable to start breeding on a large scale right from the beginning, as you still lack the necessary experience.

To obtain two healthy specimens requires the help of a good bird breeder or pet store owner. The mating pair should have good size for their variety and should have no defects. Experienced demonstrably fertile cocks can be bought. The purchaser should know the bird variety very well before making his purchase. If you are looking for color or feather structure, you have to have an experienced eye to tell a good bird from a bad bird.

Another rule for the beginner is never to mate two yellows or two buffs. Yellows give color and quality of feathers; buffs give size and substance of body and profusion of feathers. Mating two yellows will not necessarily give a more enhancing color or profusion of feathers. It would be better to mate a yellow with a buff to improve on the color and body size of a yellow.

BREEDING CAGES

Many different kinds of cages are available for breeding. A *simple cage* is used for one breeding pair. It can be constructed at home by buying a kit at your pet store or by using materials purchased at the hardware store. The simple cage is a 16" by 12" wooden frame with a wire front. The front is removable for easy cleaning. This cage usually has three perches. Two perches are placed on the back of the wooden frame so they stand vertically to the back of the cage. Another perch is placed lengthwise a few inches from the floor and stands horizontal to the viewer. Seed hoppers can be placed by the horizontal perch unless you are using an *alternate cage*.

The alternate cage is similar to the simple cage except that there are two simple cages joined by a partition. The partition is usually made out of wood for easy removal, with a wire door so the mating pair can see each other. In this way the cock is separated from the hen until she is ready to mate, and he can still sing and feed her. For multiple matings the alternate cage is also used with three or more simple cages joined with partitions separating the birds. After fertilizing one hen, the cock can be brought to mate with other hens. The seed hopper is placed by the partition.

If the simple or alternate cage is hand-built, the perches should not be too thick, as this is bad for the birds' feet. The perch should be just thick enough for the bird to grasp. A nesting box will have to be provided. This can be made of wood and should have holes for ventilation. A nest bag can be obtained from a pet shop. It is made of soft hay, moss and cowhair. When the hen is ready for mating she will begin nest-building. The nest material should not be placed in the cage too soon, as the female continues nest-building right up to the day she lays her first egg. She may continue nest-building, ripping out the nest she has already built.

In the simple cage the pair remain together during the whole breeding period. This manner of breeding has its good and bad points. Above all, the pair must show a peaceful behavior towards each other and the cock should not disturb the hen while sitting on the eggs. After the young have hatched, the cock will generally help to feed them, sometimes more actively than the female. The unfavorable points: the female proceeds to breed again sooner if the cock remains with her, sometimes while the young are still in the nest. This forces you to provide for a new nest. The female builds this up and starts to lay again. If she starts to brood, generally the fledglings still lie in the nest with her, and this may cause the eggs to be destroyed.

This variegated yellow hen and clear buff cock make a good pair of breeding Border Canaries.

A Lancashire Coppy Canary.

The *bird house* is a set-up in a room or a penthouse, males and females flying around freely in it. Their number depends on the size of the room. If you breed strains, this method is not advisable, as there is no control over which parents sired which young. In *community cages* you place one cock with three hens. This too is not advisable, as, generally, major disturbances occur with this set-up.

The most economic breeding set-up, and the presently most generalized one, is the *alternate cage.* Each female is placed in a nesting cage about 16" high by 12" long and wide. One cock services 3-4 females. It is advisable to alternate the cocks for each breeding, as you cannot foresee what the singing heredity will be. Pay attention to still another point: do not permit a cock to mate with three or four females immediately. It may happen—and it often does—that he is sterile. Therefore let the cock serve one hen and wait to see whether the eggs are fertilized. Besides this, not all females are ready to lay at the same time. Thus you do not risk the danger of a whole series of females all laying sterile eggs.

GETTING THE BREEDING STOCK AND MATERIALS

It will be best to do the following: during the summer try to get acquainted with an experienced Canary breeder who owns good breeding stock. Tell him that you wish to breed Canaries. It might be advisable to join a fanciers club, where you can receive the necessary enlightenment.

The best time to purchase breeder birds is in December. The exhibitions and prize awards are over shortly after Christmas, and you may either choose the proper breeding stock yourself, or else get someone experienced to advise you. Trust an experienced fancier in this choice, as it is difficult for a beginner. New aficionados often complain: "The supplier sold me bad stock"; "The females don't feed their young, leave the eggs, etc." Suppliers cannot sell "good" or "bad" specimens, only "healthy" or "unhealthy" birds. He himself cannot predict either whether the females will do their duty when breeding.

An experienced breeder, however, would never admit a failure in such things. Pay attention to the most important features to observe when buying Canary birds: a sound bird is slender and has smooth feathers. Hold the female in your hand, belly upturned, and blow the feathers on breast and belly apart. The breasts of healthy specimens are full-fleshed, the abdomens a little caved in, showing a small beginning of fatness. The bellies of diseased birds are red and bloated, the intestines being visible as red streaks. Such specimens are unfit for breeding. Cocks should be in full song. Sick specimens sing little or not at all.

When buying cages and accessories, consider the space you have available for them. It would be advisable to have a look at the breeding set-up of someone who has more experience. Some fanciers build their cages at home. Besides this you may sometimes buy such installations at reasonable prices from breeders who decide to stop their activities. Pet shops will probably be your best bet. They usually give breeders a special discount as they are always good potential customers.

FEEDING AND HANDLING THE STOCK UNTIL THEY START BREEDING

During winter, leave your breeder cocks at normal room temperature. If you winter them cold, there is the danger of their stopping to sing, and of their getting delayed in spring mating. The cages should not be too small. If a fancier is lucky enough to have a breeding room available, it is advisable to place the breeder cocks in the breeding cages. There the birds have sufficient opportunity to fly around, and are able fliers when breeding starts. As food use a good line of turnip seed and mixed food. Offer the birds a weekly helping of egg food mixed with ground carrots, or a piece of apple.

Be careful not to make the diet too regular. Variety in feeding never hurt anyone. We humans, too, do not like to eat the same dish day in and day out. Besides this, all specimens do not eat exactly the same quantities of food, one needing more, the other one less. Fresh water and cleanliness are self-evident musts. The bottoms of the cages should be covered with grit. Under such care and feeding, the cocks remain healthy, and will be prepared for their duty in spring.

Females are generally wintered cold, that is, one does not

A typical Canary nest with eggs.

A nest of Canary chicks about ten days old.

keep them in heated rooms. The reason for this is to be sought in the fact that, if the birds are wintered warm, on one hand they become soft, while on the other they start laying too soon. This does not mean, however, that you should expose your hen Canaries to excessive cold. The correct procedure is cold wintering in which you place the hens in an unheated room, into which little or no outside cold can penetrate. Something that should never happen to your birds are air drafts. It is not every fancier, though, who has such rooms available. In such cases it will cause no harm if you lodge the Canaries in a room where a few degrees of cold prevail. If the hen Canaries are fed right, they will withstand dry cold quite well.

The larger the breeding cage the better. If you can place the cage in a spot where it receives sufficient light, especially sunlight, this will be very useful. Feeding the breeder hens is quite different from feeding the cocks, owing both to the large flying cage and to the low temperature. The main staple is good summer rape seed. Additionally they have to receive a varied mixed food.

When to feed is your own problem. It is advisable, especially during the cold season, to serve a larger helping of the mixed food before the evening. It is also good to give some foods separate, one bowl with the rape seed, and another one with the mixed seeds. This will avoid the birds scattering food all over the cage.

Fresh water is something your birds must always have available. Except during freezing weather a daily change is sufficient. When the weather is freezing, though, you will have to change the water several times a day. Stop feeding greens and apples in freezing weather.

Another important point is a supplement of calcium compounds. For this it is enough if you serve well-washed ground shells of raw eggs. Grit, too, should be amply present. If the bird's feet are caked with dirt—which happens quite frequently —soften the mud with warm water and remove it carefully. It is not infrequent that where the fancier fails to do such cleaning, inflammations may follow. You may afford your Canaries bathing water on frost-free days without fear of consequences. Females wintered in this manner will do their duty in the breeding cages. When in March the sun shines warm again, you will notice that the birds become livelier. The mating instinct awakens, and you may now start preparations for breeding.

THE FIRST BATCH OF FLEDGLINGS

When you start breeding, adapt to nature. If breeding is done in a heated room, it may start around the middle of March. If this is not the case, you will have to wait until the April weather is fit for it. In the former case, place the females in the breeding cages during the first days of March, and get them accustomed to the warmth gradually. Sudden changes may cause health disturbances.

After the hens have been sitting in their breeding cages for a few days, and have become used to them, you may start serving breeding food. The usual food is given as before, but you may now offer a larger proportion of egg food. Why do we feed egg food? Chicken eggs contain substances which our female Canary needs to produce her own eggs.

Give a daily helping of this food, ½ teaspoon in a special little bowl, preferably in the morning. Continue feeding rape seed and mixed food as before. Pay attention to the temperature in the nesting room when you start feeding egg food. It should be between 50 and 60 degrees F.

The author serves plenty of green vegetables from the start to the end of the nesting season, with the best of success. Even if this softens the excrements a little, this is preferable to having the birds suffer from constipation. If you are lucky enough to have your breeding room face east or south, you will soon notice that the females become quite lively.

If the cocks are placed near them, and start to sing, the females will respond with loud mating calls. The mating instinct has been aroused. The hens jump around untiringly on the perches and flap their wings.

Now give them nesting material which can be bought at any well-stocked pet shop. The birds pick up a beak-full, jump around restively, and carry it to the nest and back. Soon nest building begins, and the nest may be finished within a few hours.

Two green Canaries, just weaned.

Opposite, upper photo:
These chicks being fed by the
hen are about a week old.

Opposite, lower photo:
Crested Canaries are the result of a mutation in breeding; this is an ideal example
of a crest.

Things that are "old hat" to the experienced breeder are not necessarily the same to the beginner. To begin with we have to state that many a beginner places the cock in the nesting cage as soon as he puts the female there, in the hope that the cock may mate with her. There are cases in which such experiments succeed, which means that the female is already ripe for mating. Generally, however, this is not the case, and the consequence is stormy quarrels between the pair. Since she is not yet sufficiently ripe for mating, the female will simply refuse the male. The ensuing mating battles may easily lead to damages to the pair of breeder, and it may even happen that one or the other partner may lose his or her life. In order to avoid such unfortunate happenings, the cock should only be admitted near the female at the right moment, which is when she is fully ready for mating.

As a rule the Canary hen is only ripe for mating when she starts to build her nest and when her abdomen is pear-shaped, showing a reddish inflammation near the end. When the female carries building materials to the nest, sits in it, and begins to turn and shape it, this means that you should place the cock with her on the ensuing day. In most cases you will then notice that she permits the cock to fertilize her. There are cases, however, in which even a female that is ready for mating simply does not accept the cock. In this case you will have to try a ruse: admit the cock in the evening, at twilight time. Early the next morning, at dawn, turn on the light in the nesting room, and whistle a little. In most cases the female will now submit, and a red-blooded cock will bestride her, especially an experienced one. Young, untried cocks often are too clumsy for such surprise actions. If this still should fail, you will have to try another male. Should this too prove without success, exclude the female completely from the proceedings. If she lays some unfertilized eggs, let her sit on them, and give her some young from another hen to raise. Thus she will fulfill her maternal duties, and will carry out her task at the next mating. If the pair get on well with each other, without spats; if the cock does not tear down the nest; and if the hen does not wear down the cock, you may safely leave them together until the second egg is laid. Thus you avoid disturbing the birds by constantly moving them. After the first egg is laid, remove it carefully with a teaspoon and keep it in a safe place, wrapped up in cotton. The best place to keep the egg is a flat cigar box divided into small compartments by cardboard. Each compartment is marked with the number of the nesting cage, so that you may always know the origin of the eggs. Substitute artificial eggs for the ones you remove. If you fail to do this, ensuing eggs might not be laid in the nest.

When using the simple cage it may be necessary to keep the cock in a separate cage, called a nursery, which is a small cage made of wire so the hen can still see the cock. This is one of the reasons for using the alternate cage. The male will stand by the partition and sing in an affected manner. The female displays her readiness by moving briskly every time the male sings. The female may pull feathers from her breast as an indication of nest-building. At this time it is best to put some of the nesting material in the cage; if you don't, the female is likely to go right on plucking herself. The male will also bring offerings of food to the female, who will accept them through the partition. About this time the partition should be left open and mating should occur.

FEEDING AND HANDLING THE FLEDGLINGS

A breeder shows his real skill when handling the freshly fledged young. The young should not be weaned too soon, as they cannot eat grain if their beaks are too soft to shell it. They eat only egg food, with the consequence that they start having digestive disturbances which soon develop into intestinal diseases and eating mania. Such specimens generally cannot be cured and are lost to the fancier. You have two alternatives in order to get the birds use to rape seed. You may either soak the seed in clean water or else you may serve it shelled. Soaked rape seed has the disadvantage of easily getting covered with mildew and thus causing diseases. You will have to soak a fresh quantity for every day's feeding, and will have to remove the leftovers every night. But the birds like it a lot. Shredded rape seed is mixed with a little egg food and served this way. They never seem able to get enough of this kind of food. Offer them fresh water for drinking and bathing every day. After a few days put in some of the usual other seeds too. If the birds take and shell

Eight-week-old Border Fancies.

Opposite, upper photo:
A breeding pair of Norwich Canaries; a
clear buff cock and a variegated yellow
hen.

Opposite, lower photo:
A pair of Border Canaries displaying
typical breeding behavior.

them, your birds will have graduated to eating grain. Beside all these seeds, also feed them some shelled oats, which should be a little shredded, and also some hemp seed. Egg food, which will have to be given during the whole summer, is now served in small quantities. Whenever possible, serve it in an elongated container, so that many birds may eat simultaneously. Egg food is best given in the morning or the afternoon. If the weather is mild, give a daily helping of greens. As was mentioned before, for this we use lettuce, spinach, the shoots of dandelions and scarlet pimpernel, the latter with as many seed pods as possible. You will notice that the birds eat the seeds first. Greens should be fed in a dry and clean state, and moderately. Nestling food, available at your pet shop, is usually very satisfactory.

The eggs from the first nesting may be put back on the third evening, as in first nestings the eggs generally number a total of four. Since it was subject to brooding for the same time, the fourth egg will hatch together with the others. On the second brooding put back four eggs, as the second laying generally is more vigorous. The number of eggs per nesting varies from 3 to 6. The last, or end egg, is recognized by its darker color. It also happens frequently, especially during the first laying, that the female skips a day between eggs. This is a natural process: eggs cannot always develop that fast.

LAYING DIFFICULTY

Laying difficulty is quite a problem. It may appear for the first egg, or for later ones. On the preceding evening the hen shows that something is wrong. She sits on her perch, with the plumage fluffed up, and breathing heavily. The next morning she can hardly reach her nest, the eyes are small, and the bird can barely keep her balance. She leaves the nest frequently, and finally sits sleeping in it or in a corner of the cage. This is the moment when you must intervene. As a start, splash some drops of cold water on her inflamed abdomen. This may revitalize the muscles of the oviduct, expelling the egg. Should the remedy fail, however, try warmth. Place the little pet in a small cage, expose it to steam for a few minutes, and then place it near a heater. This will generally bring success. Operations hardly ever succeed. It may frequently take until noon until the egg is expelled, and you will be amazed at how quickly the Canary recovers. Frequently, though, laying difficulty leads to death.

After the complaint is relieved, the subsequent eggs generally are sterile. This disorder is mostly caused by strong fluctuations of temperature. Furthermore it appears most frequently during the first mating. Weakened, or too fat females, too, are prone to it, healthy and vigorous hens being rarely subject to this complaint.

BROODING AND HATCHING THE YOUNG

Once she sits on her eggs, the female begins to brood. During the brooding period besides rape seed she should also receive some mixed food, and every third or fourth day a pinch of egg food. If you feed only rape seed during the setting, and you suddenly give mixed food and egg food after the young have hatched, this may easily cause digestive disturbances in the females. You will often observe that the setting females turn around in the nest, or do things to the eggs with their bills. This is only natural, and need not worry you: the mother turns the eggs, which has to be done several times a day in order to have them all incubated evenly.

During the incubation period you will have to decide whether to remove the cock or not. Usually the hen will not notice if the cock is removed. However, some hens may not sit the full incubation time or may be poor mothers when the eggs hatch. Keeping the cock during incubation can be advantageous, for he might sit on the eggs while the female feeds. On the other hand, he may become troublesome and break the eggs. Sometimes he will begin singing and try to lure the female away from the eggs for mating. In this case the cock should be removed. If an alternating cage is used the male will perch by the partition and sing to the female, and she may leave the eggs. So if the cock is removed he must be placed out of sight of the female. As a general rule the cock is removed; only the experienced breeder can tell what his mating pair will do. Some breeders using an alternating cage with three or more com-

A slate fawn Canary (left) and a piebald spotted fawn Canary (right).

Opposite:
A beautiful clear yellow
border canary.

partments will close off the brooding hen and try to get the cock to mate with another hen.

After 4-5 days of incubation you will be able to know whether the eggs are fertile or not. Take out an egg with a teaspoon and hold it up against the light. Fertile eggs are opaque, while sterile ones are clear and transparent. An experienced breeder will notice this even while the eggs are still in the nest. The best, though, is to wait without disturbing the female. A special "don't" is touching the eggs with your fingers and removing them from the nest. Canary eggs have a very thin and brittle shell. A teaspoon will help you to avoid mishaps!

The incubation period lasts 13 to 14 days. It may happen, however, that it extends longer, since some hen Canaries do not sit very firmly during the first days. Therefore don't be impatient and open the eggs, or, what would be worse still, try to help the young to get out of their shells. This will only harm them. Young that find it difficult to leave the egg, or which cannot do this at all, are weak specimens, and will probably die anyway. After the young have hatched, check the nest for mites. The best way to check is to take out the contents and to place the nest in a hot oven for some minutes. Dry heat kills all mites. After this, let the nest cool off, and hang it back in its place. If mites suck the young intensively during the first night, you will lose them.

Don't get anxious if the female does not feed the young very much during the first days; the young still have some food in their yolk sack. If you should have the bad luck of only one or two young hatching, do not remove all other eggs immediately, but leave one or two of them in the nest. Thus the female cannot sit too heavily on the young, smothering or crippling them.

The young start growing visibly when 4-5 days old. Put the identification rings on them on the sixth to eighth day. Do not feed too much egg food during the first days, placing more emphasis on rape seed and mixed food. Start on the egg food after the young are some days old. The nestlings grow all their feathers by the eighteenth to twenty-first day, when they generally leave the nest. In most cases the female will now start building the nest for the next brood. If you have no substitute nest ready, clean the old one thoroughly.

The young must be at least 28 days old before they can be safely separated from the mother. If you are able to leave them with her for a few days more, this will only be of advantage. Too early weaned specimens are prone to great dangers. Therefore never be hasty!

If the female has completed her new nest in the time feeding the young allows her, don't miss the moment of putting the cock in with her again. In most cases she will accept him immediately, and laying takes place much quicker than for the first brood. Mating is not necessary after the first egg has been laid, as all eggs of the present batch are already fertilized. Pay special attention to the following: many cocks attack the young on sight and may kill them. Others feed them. Many young, too, fly on their fathers, and may disturb the mating act. The best thing to do is to remove the offspring for a short time, in order to avoid quarrels and strife. The second brooding takes place in a manner that is similar to the first one. Separate the fledglings as to sexes and place them in flying cages, after both broodings are completed.

SEXING THE YOUNG CANARIES

As soon as you take out the fledglings which have grown independent, separate them as to sex. How will you know the cocks from the hens, though? An infallible sign is singing. Just a few days after leaving the nest, while the mother still feeds them, the young males frequently sit like they are in a trance, whip their tails, and softly squeeze out a few more or less connected sounds from their little throats. Such sounds—they could hardly be called song—are never heard from the females. The older the cocks grow, the louder and harder they "sing."

A blue variegated white Yorkshire Canary.

Bird Shows

I cannot end this little book without a short word on bird shows, having been interested in them for a number of years.

There are various shows in all parts of the country, usually beginning in October and continuing until about Christmas. There are a few in January.

Some shows are only for Red Factor Canaries, some only for Roller Canaries and some have sections for type birds. Each variety has its own standard show cage and way of being prepared for the show. They are judged by qualified judges and awards are made. Sometimes the competition becomes very interesting.

Two variegated Gloster Fancy Canaries with typical dark coronas.

If you like birds you might be interested in attending a show. If you are interested in buying a bird it will give you a chance to see the different varieties and thus know which would appeal to you personally. Or you may want to enter your own Canary in a show.

Teaching a Roller to sing or a Norwich to pose requires training when the bird is young. The show cage should be introduced when the bird is just weaned. The show cage is placed next to the bird's regular cage with both doors left open, allowing the bird access to the show cage. When the Canary has gained confidence in the show cage it should be taught to enter on command. Usually a training stick is used to avoid handling. After it has learned to enter the show cage the bird will be taught to assume position or to sing on command. To teach a bird to pose, the trainer usually scratches with his training stick or finger and uses his voice to coax the bird to assume the right position or to sing. This requires much patience and training while the bird is young, but it is very rewarding.

A traveling cage will be needed to transport your Canary to the bird show. Traveling cages must be light and sturdy. They are obtainable from most pet suppliers and usually made of plywood. Whether traveling or not, the bird will usually have to be hand-washed for show. Most bird societies arrange a demonstration of hand-washing, and most fanciers will be able to show you. Hand-washing is done a few days before show to allow the plumage to fluff up.

Most of the Canaries in the United States came from British stock. In Great Britain there are three major interests: singing varieties, body conformation and color. The rating scale used in this country is much the same as is used in Great Britain, with the exception of the American Singer Canary. The usual judging is according to class. The classes are Old Cock, Young Cock, Old Hen and Young Hen. The rating is in points according to the Canary variety, so a Roller is judged on a point system as to song and a Yorkshire is judged as to color and feather proportion. Each bird is judged on its own merit according to an ideal standard and is awarded more points the closer it comes to the ideal standard. The American Singer Canary is a special breed of Canary developed in America especially for song. It is 70 per cent Roller and 30 per cent Border Fancy. American Singers compete against one another in a bird show. The American Singer is to sing freely despite commotion, so after he is moved from the stands to the judging bench the bird has ten minutes in which to perform for the judge. If the bird does not sing, he is eliminated.

In the United States, people who become active in showing their Canaries subscribe to *American Cage-Bird Magazine* (3449 North Western Ave., Chicago, Illinois 60618) which has monthly listings of Canary specialty clubs and bird shows. In the United Kingdom, the Foreign Bird League publishes the highly interesting magazine *Foreign Birds* (131 Berridge Road East, Sherwood Rise, Nottingham); two Australian bird societies, the Avicultural Society of Australia (10 Tyne Street, Burwood, Victoria 3125) and The Avicultural Society of South Australia (17 Benjamin St., Hampstead, South Australia) can be of help to Canary fanciers.

Other good T.F.H. Publications Canary books that you might enjoy, depending on your degree of experience in the Canary Fancy, are:

> **Stroud's Diseases of Canaries,** by Robert Stroud (the Birdman of Alcatraz); T.F.H. Publications style number PS-640.

> **Encyclopedia of Canaries,** by G.T. Dodwell. T.F.H. Publications style number H-967.

> **Canaries for Pleasure and Profit,** by Cliff Newby. T.F.H. Publications style number AP-270.

In addition to the above-listed books, a very useful text is the expensive but brilliant treatise **Bird Diseases**, by Drs. L. Arnall and I.F. Keymer. T.F.H. Publications style number H-964. This is not a canary specialtiy book but an all-around useful text providing insight into bird physiology and the treatment of diseases of birds.

These books are available for inspection and purchase at pet shops and book stores everywhere.